OCS Study MMS 2006-032

Final Report

CODAR in Alaska

Principal Investigator: Dave Musgrave, PhD
Associate Professor
School of Fisheries and Ocean Sciences
University of Alaska Fairbanks
P.O. Box 757220
Fairbanks, AK 99775-7220
(907) 474-7837
musgrave@ims.uaf.edu

CoAuthor: Hank Statscewich, MS
School of Fisheries and Ocean Sciences
University of Alaska Fairbanks
P.O. Box 757220
Fairbanks, AK 99775-7220
(907) 474-5720
stats@ims.uaf.edu

June 2006

Table of Contents

List of Tables

List of figures

Abstract

From December 2002 through June 2003, surface currents were measured and analyzed near the mouth of the Kenai River in upper Cook Inlet (Figure 1). This was achieved by utilizing High Frequency (HF) radar systems manufactured by Coastal Ocean Dynamic Applications Radar (CODAR) Ocean Sensors, which operated continuously, aside from a seven-day dropout of data due to a damaged computer modem. Spatial coverage of the data return varied over the semidiurnal tidal period due to exposed beach seaward of the radar antennas during low tides, and over subtidal frequencies spatial coverage was reduced during periods of no or slight winds, presumably due to the absence of significant energy in the wave field at the Bragg wavelength. Tidal currents accounted for about 90% of the total current variance, and tidal ellipses for all tidal components were polarized along the axis of the inlet. The dominant component was the lunar semidiurnal (M2), with major axis magnitudes ranging from $30 - 200$ cm s^{-1}. Mean subtidal currents were as great as 25 cm s^{-1}, and the current patterns were related to the wind direction.

Particle excursions due to tides are between $4 - 32$ km in this section of Cook Inlet, and predicted tidal current ellipses agree quite well in magnitude and phase with the tidal model of Foreman *et al.* (2000).

Comparison of surface velocities from the HF radar with drifters drogued at 7 m gave root-mean-square (rms) differences in the range of $40 - 100$ cm s^{-1}. The large differences are probably due to large vertical shear in the upper 7 m of the water column.

Introduction

Electromagnetic remote sensing of ocean currents from the shoreline using HF radar provides a complete mapping capability that has become a cost-effective solution for coastal current mapping. This technique was developed more than three decades ago and has received wide acceptance in the oceanographic community. Currently, there are approximately 150 of these instruments used around the world for the purpose of measuring ocean currents. HF radar formally spans the frequency range of 3 – 30 MHz (with wavelengths between 10 m at the upper end and 100 m at the lower end). A vertically polarized HF signal propagated along the electrically conductive ocean water surface can travel well beyond the line-of-sight, where more common microwave radars become blind. Rain or fog does not affect HF signals.

Over the past 25 years, oceanographic radar techniques have been developed and improved so that detailed, gridded, two-dimensional maps of surface circulation can be provided and recorded in real time (Barrick 1978, Prandle 1989). Currents play a critical role in the transport and fate of spilled oil, but there is a paucity of direct circulation measurements in some areas of Cook Inlet. Current meters provide data at only a few specific points and not at the water surface, where the oil would be found. HF radar techniques provide a measured equivalent of a gridded circulation model and can be used as input and validation for oil spill trajectory models. The accuracy of the surface current measurements has been reported to be between 4 – 20 cm s^{-1}

These systems operate by transmitting a low power (40 watt average) radio signal frequency from land, which is reflected in all directions by the surface wave field. In accordance with Bragg scattering theory, reflected electromagnetic (em) waves that are exactly one-half the wavelength of the transmitted em waves add constructively to give a peak in radiation. This reflected Bragg peak is Doppler shifted in frequency by the combined effects of ocean waves and ocean currents. Utilizing well known wave dispersion theory, the speed of the surface gravity wave is subtracted from the total speed measured by the HF radar instrumentation. The resulting quantity represents the component of the surface ocean current which is traveling in a radial direction, either toward or away, from the transceiver. HF radar systems use radial components from at least two sites to determine the total current vector at a given point.

The physical oceanography of Cook Inlet, Alaska, is characterized by complex circulation associated with variability at tidal, seasonal, annual and interannual time scales. As this region has the fourth largest tidal range in the world, the circulation is dominated by tidally driven flows with current speeds of up to 300 cm s^{-1} (6 knots). Knowledge of the tidal and sub-tidal current patterns in Cook Inlet is essential for determining and predicting transport pathways affecting pollutants. In this study, surface currents measured by HF radar instrumentation are used to characterize the circulation of the area and assess the skill of numerical simulations of this system.

Middle Cook Inlet is a dynamic region with significant sub-tidal circulation, including a south flowing buoyancy driven current along the western shore (Johnson and Okkonen, 2000). The bathymetry of the region is characterized by two 50 – 100 m deep troughs located in the center of the inlet and on the western side of Kalgin Island (Figure 2).

This study's objectives were to investigate the utility of using HF radar in Cook Inlet for measuring surface currents. In addition, bistatic systems were investigated as a potential less expensive alternative to the monostatic system that we deployed.

Methods

An array of two Seasondes (CODAR Ocean Sensors' HF radar systems) measured hourly surface currents near the mouth of the Kenai River on the eastern shore of Cook Inlet. The systems were deployed in December 2002 and operated until June 2003. Each site consisted of a transmit antenna, a receive antenna, radar electronics and a computer for control and data logging. The radar electronics were housed in heated structures near the antennas and were powered by utilizing electricity from nearby private homes. The antennas were located as close to the ocean as possible, less than 100 meters from the sea surface, to minimize signal attenuation by propagation over land. Unfortunately, at low tide long stretches of wetted sand were exposed during periods of large tidal fluctuations at the southern Seasonde site (Site 2, Kalifornski Beach). Signal attenuation during these periods was large and contributed to fluctuations in the spatial coverage of this radar unit.

Extremely accurate GPS time synchronization permitted the two radar units to transmit concurrently at 13.51 MHz. At this frequency the transmitted signal has a wavelength of 22 m, yielding a wavelength (λ) of the surface Bragg waves of 11 m.

The Bragg scattering effect results in two discrete, well defined peaks in the Doppler spectrum. In the absence of any ocean current, the position of these echo peaks is symmetric and their frequency is given by

$$f_B = \pm \frac{2C_0}{\lambda}$$

where $C_0 = \sqrt{(g\lambda/2\pi)}$ is the linear phase speed of the surface Bragg wave in deep water and g is the acceleration due to gravity. A current underlying the surface waves causes a translation of the entire coordinate frame with respect to a stationary observer or shore based radar stations. Thus the Bragg peaks in the Doppler spectra are displaced from the Bragg frequency f_B by an amount

$$\Delta f = 2V_r / \lambda$$

where V_r is the radial component of the effective surface current along the look direction of the radar.

Backscattered radar signals are Doppler shifted by an amount proportional to the intrinsic deep water phase velocity of 11 m ocean waves. Radial ocean current velocities are then found by calculating the difference between the measured and the intrinsic phase velocities. This difference corresponds to the average current from the surface to a depth of order $\lambda/4\pi$ (Stewart and Joy 1974), or approximately 90 cm at 13 MHz transmit frequency. Two-dimensional surface currents can be computed by geometrically combining the components along radar beams emanating from two radar stations using the method described by Graber et al. (1997).

Range to a sector of ocean surface is determined using frequency modulation, which divides the coverage area into concentric circular arcs called range cells. As implemented by CODAR Ocean Sensors, Ltd., the Multiple Signal Classification (MUSIC) based processing algorithm divides these range cells into azimuthal sectors of ocean surface and estimates the currents in each sector (Schmidt 1986; Barrick and Lipa 1997). Each sector collected hourly current measurements at 1.5 km in range and 5° in bearing. The coverage of the systems typically extended 40 km and across the inlet to Kalgin Island. In contrast to *in situ* sensors, which essentially measure currents at a point, the sector areas associated with HF radar vary linearly from $0.2 - 5.5$ km^2 as range varies from $1.5 - 40$ km. Current measurements represent an average of surface currents within the sector area. More precisely, the HF radar current estimates are based upon all of the spectral information obtained within the resolved area. Horizontal variations in the current field with scale lengths less than 1.5 km will result in broadened or multiple Doppler spectral peaks. A detailed discussion of the MUSIC processing algorithm and its limitations may be found in

Emery et al. 2004. In the case of the Cook Inlet study, Doppler spectra are computed every 10 minutes and then processed to produce radial current estimates. The 10-min radial current data are then averaged to produce hourly radial vectors for each sector. The 256-point transform used to estimate cross spectra limits the radial speed resolution to 4 cm s^{-1}.

Measurements of meteorological variables were obtained from two sensors located within the HF radar coverage area. The Drift River station is operated by the National Data Buoy Center (NDBC). Hourly averaged measurements of wind speed and direction, air temperature, barometric pressure and dew point are available from the NDBC website. The National Oceanographic and Atmospheric Administration (NOAA) National Ocean Service (NOS) division operates another meteorological and tide gauging station in Nikiski, AK. Measurements found on the NOAA NOS website provide wind speed and direction, air temperature, barometric pressure and water level for Nikiski.

We compared estimates of surface velocities from the surface current mappers with drifting buoys deployed in this area by Dr. Mark Johnson (UAF). Details of the design, deployment, processing of the data from the drifters can be found at http://www.ims.uaf.edu/research/johnson/cmi/cookinletbuoys.html.

Results

Spatial and Temporal Coverage

An overall indicator of radar performance is spatial coverage over time. Coverage is defined as the number of sectors returning radials each hour. Since a two site radar network is required to produce two-dimensional surface current maps, we modify the definition of coverage to represent data recovery in a two-dimensional sense. In order to transform radial currents to vector maps, a rectangular grid is defined which extends throughout the maximum possible coverage area. Vector estimates were then attempted for each grid location using a least squares vector fit (Lipa and Barrick, 1983), which was applied to all data within a radius of 3 km. An average is calculated and mapped onto the grid. These mapped vectors represent the "raw" data used in this study. Thus coverage is defined as the number of grid points where vector currents are measured. The hypothetical coverage area under which total vectors may be created is shown in Figure 3. In this figure small dots represent total vector grid points and contour lines represent the Geometric Dilution of Precision (GDOP) assumed when calculating a total vector from two radials (Chapman et al. 1997). GDOP is an amplification factor of the error estimate placed on a particular vector current measurement. These errors arise as the angle of incidence between two radial currents deviates from 90°, as the ability to resolve perpendicular velocity components is not possible along the baseline of the two radial sites.

Gaps in the time series of vector currents arise when there were insufficient radial data nearby to estimate the vector current. Gaps in the radial data occur when: (1) the MUSIC direction finding algorithm cannot resolve all angular directions for a given range cell, (2) low signal to noise ratios cause an inability to discern Bragg sea echo, usually resulting in range fluctuations, and (3) the system is down. There were many data gaps caused by the first two reasons, but the third was not much of an issue as both sites operated 95% of the time during the experiment. There was one major

power outage on the Kenai Peninsula on March 28, 2003, which caused two failures within the northern radar system. The first was a power surge in the telephone line which damaged the computer modem, and the second was a total discharge of the Uninterruptible Power Supply (UPS) connected to the radar electronics. A new modem and UPS were installed at this site, but the failures caused a loss of data for 7 consecutive days. The coverage ranged from no data during times of very low tides with no winds to excellent (Figure 4).

The number of current measurements collected over any single hour in the Cook Inlet HF radar study area varies from 0 – 1200 (Figure 4). Since propagation of the HF radar radio ground wave relies on seawater as a conductive medium, coverage is modulated by the extent of land the radio signal must travel over before reaching seawater. Time series of coverage, sea-level and wind speed from Nikiski indicate that there is a strong correlation between environmental conditions and system performance. First, at semidiurnal frequencies there is a high squared coherence ($\gamma^2 = 0.9$) between coverage and water level due to the significant amount of exposed beach at low tide. This is similar to the findings of Emery *et al.* (2004) although their coverage variations were expressed at diurnal frequencies. Variations resulted in patchiness and fluctuations in range as observed by Prandle *et al.* (1993) and Paduan and Rosenfeld (1996). Furthermore, high squared coherence ($\gamma^2 = 0.8$) exists at a 2.5 day period between the number of totals and wind speed, suggesting that higher wind speeds create a more favorable environment for the HF system at 12 MHz.

Tidal Variability

In the following discussions, we used data from the grid (Figure 3) that had greater than 50% coverage over the entire period of operation. The matlab program "t_tide" (Pawlowicz et al., 2002) was used at each grid point in the domain to calculate the tidal constituents. Table 1 shows the results for one point near the center of the domain. Tidal currents are dominated by the M2 tidal constituent with current magnitudes ranging from 30 – 200 cm s^{-1}. Tidal currents account for approximately 66 – 95% of the total current variance with a mean of 89%. Due to the strong north-south polarization of the tidal currents, only 67% (mean over the domain) of the variance is predicted in the longitudinal (east-west) direction; however 90% of the variance is predicted in the meridional direction. Tidal current ellipses (Figure 5) for the four major tidal constituents reveal a strong polarization of tidal currents in the north-south direction, consistent with steering by local bathymetry and orientation of Cook Inlet. The magnitudes are generally greater and more polarized in the mid inlet region than near the sides for all constituents. Particle excursion distances, $\delta = U * T / \pi$, where U is the magnitude of the major axis and T the period, are between 4 and 32 km. Tidal analyses over monthly periods have similar results.

Subtidal Variability

For analysis of subtidal flows, a 33 hour filter was applied to time series of data at each grid point (Beardsley et. al, 1983). The mean flow over the whole period is shown in Figure 6a. The mean wind stress (actually pseudo-wind stress which is the magnitude squared in the direction of the wind) measured at Drift River is northerly (blowing from the north) and is aligned with the axis of Cook Inlet. The current pattern shows persistent southward currents along the northeast side of Kalgin Island with speeds up to 25 cm s^{-1}, northward currents in the center of the Inlet and southward flow near Site 2 in the eastern Inlet. The monthly averaged currents all show the persistent southward flow along Kalgin Island, but when the winds are strong in a southward direction (Figure 6b), the northward flow in the center of the Inlet is decreased, and the southerly flow near Site 2 is greater. When the winds are reversed (Figure 6c), the mid inlet northward flow is greater and

the southward flow near Site 2 is less. While subtidal current speeds are significantly weaker than tidal currents, they may dominate transport processes at time scales longer than the dominant tidal periods due to their persistence.

The principal axes of the subtidal current variability are polarized along the axis of the inlet with major axis magnitudes ranging between 20 and 40 cm s^{-1} (Figure 7). The principal axes are more polarized in midinlet.

Model verification

Tidal predictions from HF radar instrumentation are used to assess the accuracy of the Foreman (2000) barotropic numerical tide model for the region. Differences between the major axes of HF radar derived and modeled tidal current ellipses fall into the range of 0.6 – 24 cm s^{-1} and phase differences are between 35° and 234° (Table 2). Large discrepancies between the tidal constituent parameters from the model may be a result of inadequate representation of the complex bathymetry of the region.

HF Radar – Drifter Comparisons

Three current-following drifters were deployed in the coverage area of the HF radar instrumentation during the study and persisted in the area for periods ranging from 2 – 4 weeks (Figure 8). The drifters were of a holey sock design and were deployed in the vicinity of the central tide rip at the deepest section of the inlet, drouged 10 m below the surface. Collocated HF radar surface current measurements show a high degree of scatter with RMS velocity differences in the range of 40 – 100 cm s^{-1} (Figure 9). Vertical shear in the water column due to the presence of strong stratification appears to limit the usefulness of extrapolating full water column velocities from surface current measurements in Cook Inlet. Relatively large differences in the drifter-HF radar velocities may skew these average statistics (Figure 10).

Discussion

As expected, tidal currents dominate the flows in Cook Inlet and account for about 70 – 90% of the total variance. All variability (tidal and subtidal) is polarized along the axis of the inlet. Patterns of mean surface currents show across inlet variability with (generally) southward flow in the west, a reversal of flow in mid inlet and southward flow in the east, although winds can affect this pattern.

Comparison of Foreman's tidal model (2000) with the HF radar-derived tidal constituents shows good agreement, while the agreement between drifters drogued at 10 m and the HF radar surface currents is poor due to large vertical shears.

References

Barrick, D.E. 1978. HF radio oceanography – A review. Bound.-Lay. Meteorol. 13(1–4):23–43. doi: 10.1007/BF00913860

Barrick, D.E., and B.J. Lipa. 1997. Evolution of bearing determination in HF current mapping radars. Oceanography 10(2):72–75.

Beardsley, R.C., R. Limeburner and L.K. Rosenfeld. 1985. Introduction to the CODE-2 moored array and large-scale data report. *In* R. Limeburner [ed.], CODE-2: Moored Array and Large-Scale Data Report. Woods Hole Oceanographic Institution Technical Report No. 38, WHOI-85-35.

Chapman, R.D., L.K. Shay, H.C. Graber, J.B. Edson, A. Karachintsev, C.L. Trump and D.B. Ross. 1997. On the accuracy of HF radar surface current measurements: Intercomparisons with ship-based sensors. J. Geophys. Res. 102(C8):18,737–18,748. doi: 10.1029/97JC00049

Emery, B.M., L. Washburn and J.A. Harlan. 2004. Evaluating radial current measurements from CODAR high-frequency radars with moored current meters. J. Atmos. Ocean. Tech. 21(8):1259–1271. doi: 10.1175/1520-0426(2004)021<1259:ERCMFC>2.0.CO;2

Foreman, M.G.G., W.R. Crawford, J.Y. Cherniawsky, R.F. Henry and M.R. Tarbotton. 2000. A high-resolution assimilating tidal model for the northeast Pacific Ocean. J. Geophys. Res. 105(C12):28,629–28,652. doi: 10.1029/1999JC000122

Graber, H.C., B.K. Haus, R.D. Chapman and L.K. Shay. 1997. HF radar comparisons with moored estimates of current speed and direction: Expected differences and implications. J. Geophys. Res. 102(C8):18,749–18,766. doi: 10.1029/97JC01190

Johnson, M.A., and S.R. Okkonen [eds.]. 2000. Proceedings Cook Inlet Oceanography Workshop. November 1999, Kenai, Alaska. Final Report. OCS Study MMS 2000-043, University of Alaska Coastal Marine Institute, University of Alaska Fairbanks and USDOI, MMS, Alaska OCS Region, 118 p.

Lipa, B.J., and D.E. Barrick. 1983. Least-squares method for the extraction of surface currents from CODAR crossed-loop data: Application at ARSLOE. IEEE J. Oceanic Eng. 8(4):226–253.

Paduan, J.D., and L.K. Rosenfeld. 1996. Remotely sensed surface currents in Monterey Bay from shore-based HF radar (Coastal Ocean Dynamics Application Radar). J. Geophys. Res. 101(C9):20,669–20,686. doi: 10.1029/96JC01663

Pawlowicz, R., B. Beardsley and S. Lentz. 2002. Classical tidal harmonic analysis including error estimates in MATLAB using T_TIDE. Computers and Geosciences. 28(8):929–937. doi: 10.1016/S0098-3004(02)00013-4

Prandle, D., and D.K. Ryder. 1989. Comparison of observed (HF radar) and modelled nearshore velocities. Cont. Shelf Res. 9(11):941–963. doi: 10.1016/0278-4343(89)90001-0

Prandle, D., S.G. Loch and R. Player. 1993. Tidal flow through the Straits of Dover. J. Phys. Oceanogr. 23(1):23–37. doi: 10.1175/1520-0485(1993)023<0023:TFTTSO>2.0.CO;2

Schmidt, R.O. 1986. Multiple emitter location and signal parameter estimation. IEEE Trans. Antenn. Propag. 34(3):276–280.

Stewart, R.H., and J.W. Joy. 1973. HF radio measurements of ocean currents, p. 64–67. *In* Proceedings IEEE International Conference on Engineering in the Ocean Environment, 25–28 September, Seattle, Washington.

Table 1: Tidal Current Parameters for a single CODAR grid point.

Tidal Constituent	Period (hours)	Major Axis (cm s^{-1})	Minor Axis (cm s^{-1})	Inclination (deg) of the major axis	Phase (deg, relative to UTC)	Signal to Noise Ratio
M2	12.42081729	126.962	-14.697	88.52	322.98	66
S2	12.00048002	26.555	1.954	75.89	310.3	3.1
K2	11.96744854	23.023	1.694	75.89	245.21	2.3
K1	23.93489708	14.737	1.007	82.93	193.85	24
N2	12.65822785	10.931	2.33	97.85	301.25	0.5
P	24.06738869	9.554	0.653	82.93	245.82	10
O1	25.81977795	6.349	-0.874	80.56	235.88	4.5
Q1	26.86727566	1.671	0.242	109.7	311	0.33

Table 2: Bulk tidal ellipse parameters from observations (HF radar), model results (Foreman) and the difference between the two.

Tidal Constituent	Period (hours)		Major Axis (cm s^{-1})	Minor Axis (cm s^{-1})	Phase (deg)	Inclination (deg)
M2	12.4206	HF radar	102.3536	8.7606	-37.9433	76.8797
		Foreman	126.7034	7.6395	-13.0339	76.1858
		Foreman - radar	24.3498	-1.1212	24.9094	-0.6939
S2	12.0005	HF radar	23.8658	0.831	-47.1677	72.7341
		Foreman	45.4339	2.7879	24.7659	76.1949
		Foreman - radar	21.5681	1.9569	71.9337	3.4608
K2	11.9672	HF radar	20.6916	0.7205	-112.2577	72.7341
		Foreman	10.6274	0.6643	15.9802	76.9211
		Foreman - radar	-10.0642	-0.0561	128.2379	4.187
K1	23.9345	HF radar	12.555	0.9161	-175.9291	74.467
		Foreman	17.1127	0.8856	59.0164	-99.6886
		Foreman - radar	4.5578	-0.0304	234.9455	-174.1556
N2	12.6583	HF radar	10.3086	0.3696	-91.1233	79.0191
		Foreman	25.6134	1.5303	-41.1007	76.2084
		Foreman - radar	15.3048	1.1607	50.0226	-2.8107
P1	24.0659	HF radar	8.1394	0.5939	-123.9591	74.467
		Foreman	2.5099	0.0609	-88.1216	70.6166
		Foreman - radar	-5.6295	-0.5329	35.8375	-3.8504
O1	25.8193	HF radar	3.7673	0.5777	-126.0075	87.1827
		Foreman	13.4784	0.6131	60.0469	-101.4094
		Foreman - radar	9.7112	0.0354	186.0545	-188.5921
Q1	26.8684	HF radar	1.404	0.1768	-74.9323	77.638
		Foreman	0.8131	0.0278	79.6649	-73.4447
		Foreman - radar	-0.5909	-0.149	154.5973	-151.0826

Instantaneous currents: 3/21/2003 21:00 UTC

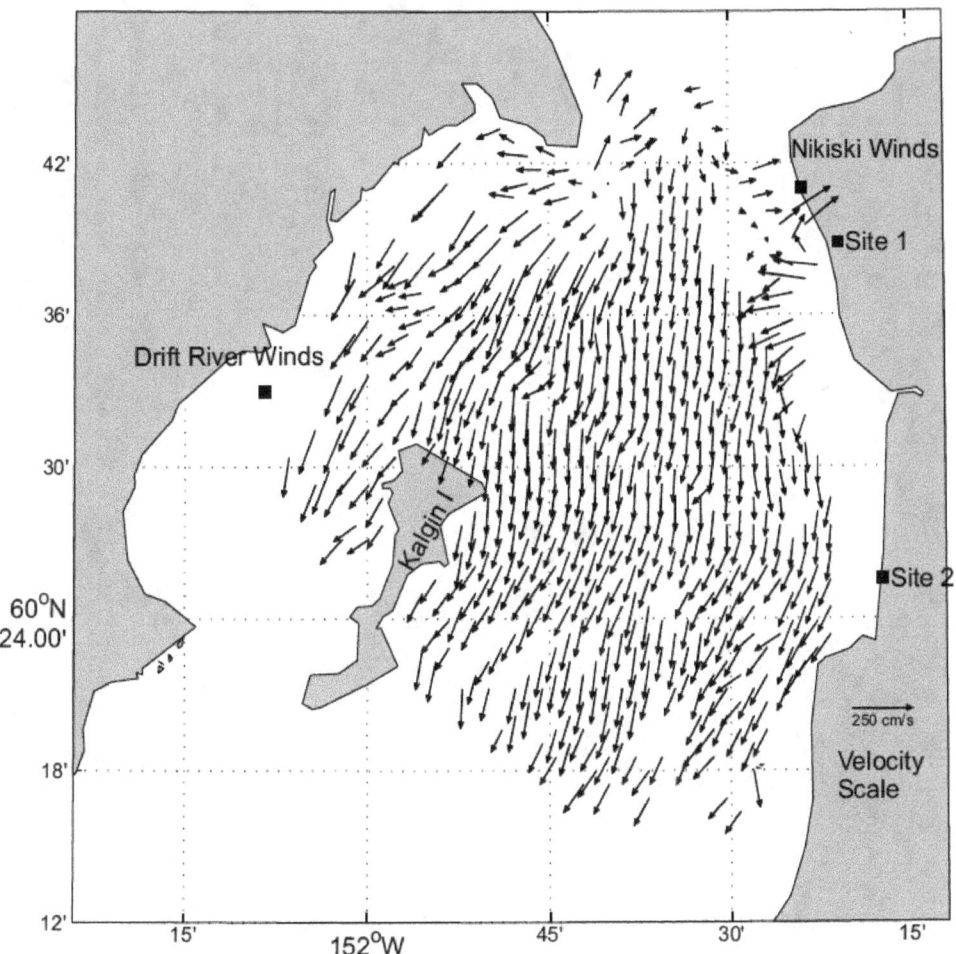

Figure 1: Study area for HF radar surface currents in Cook Inlet, Alaska. Boxes identifying Sites 1 and 2 are the locations of the HF radar systems. They are 25 km apart and are located north and south of the Kenai River. This graphic shows data from 21:00 GMT, March 21, 2003. The pointing direction of the arrows indicate the direction of flow of the surface currents, and the arrow length indicates the magnitude of the current (magnitude scale is located in the lower right corner). The region of coverage for two dimensional velocities extends more than 10 km north of Site 1, more than 10km south of Site 2, and 45 km across the inlet, with a spatial resolution of about 2 km. Locations of the Drift River and Nikiski meteorological stations are also plotted.

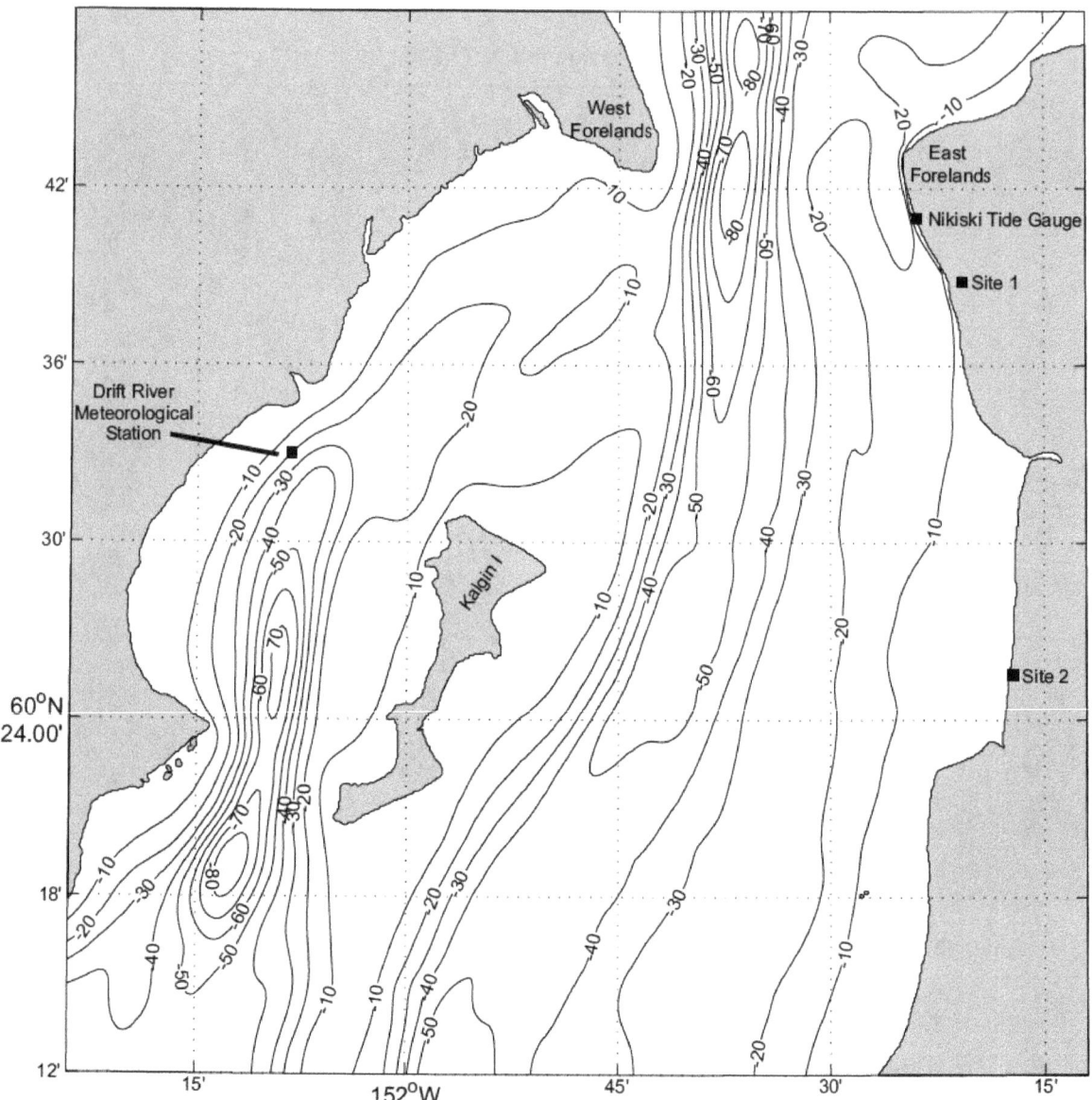

Figure 2: Map of Cook Inlet showing the bathymetry (m) of the region.

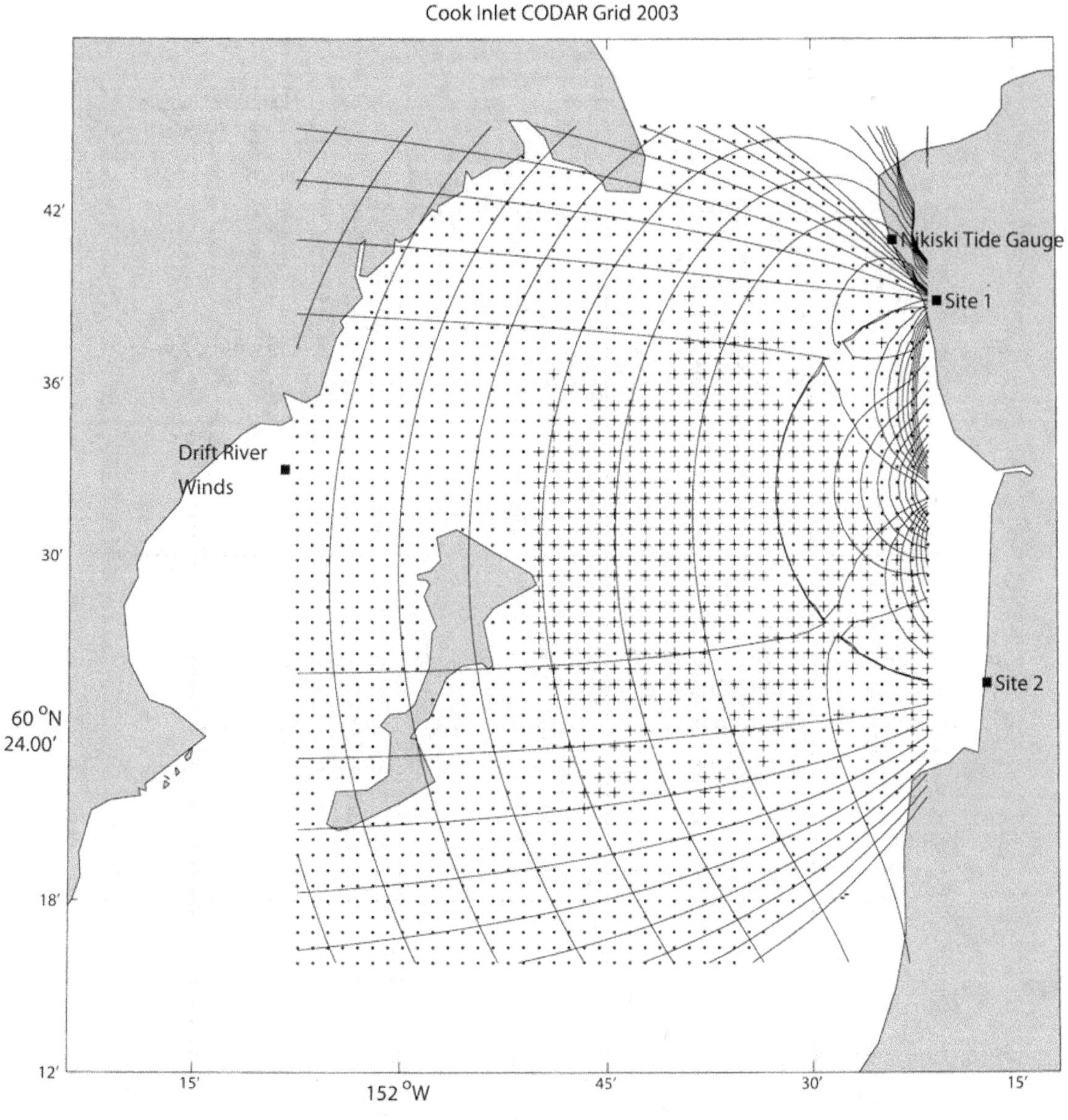

Figure 3: Map of Cook Inlet HF Radar domain. Small dots represent total vector grid points and contour lines represent the Geometric Dilution of Precision (GDOP) in both the east-west and north-south directions. The plus symbols represent grid points where total vectors were observed greater than 50% of the time and where the GDOP < 1.8.

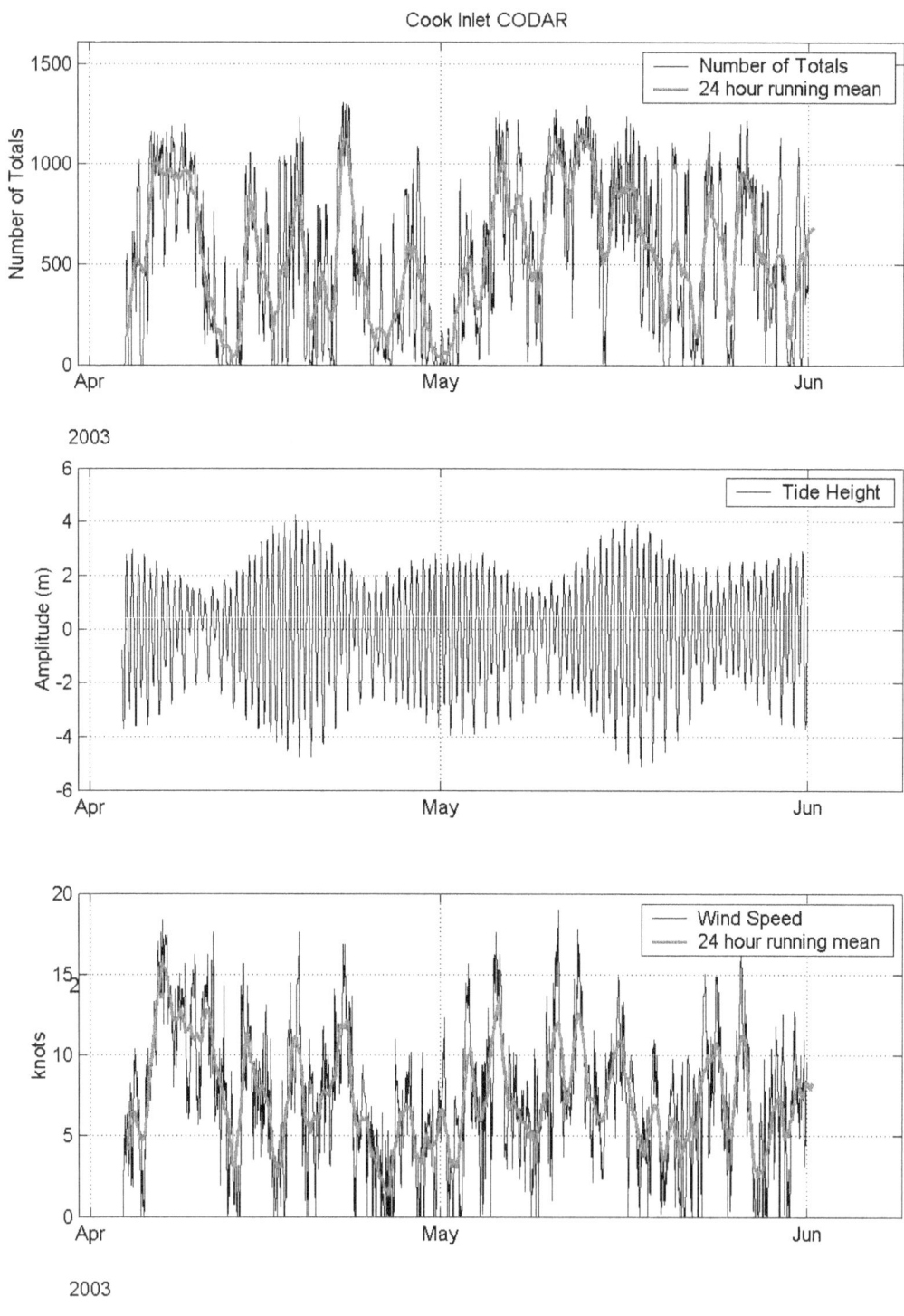

Figure 4: Raw time series of (a) the number of current vectors at the Cook Inlet HF radar array (b) the tidal height amplitude from the Nikiski tide gauge and (c) wind speed from Nikiski.

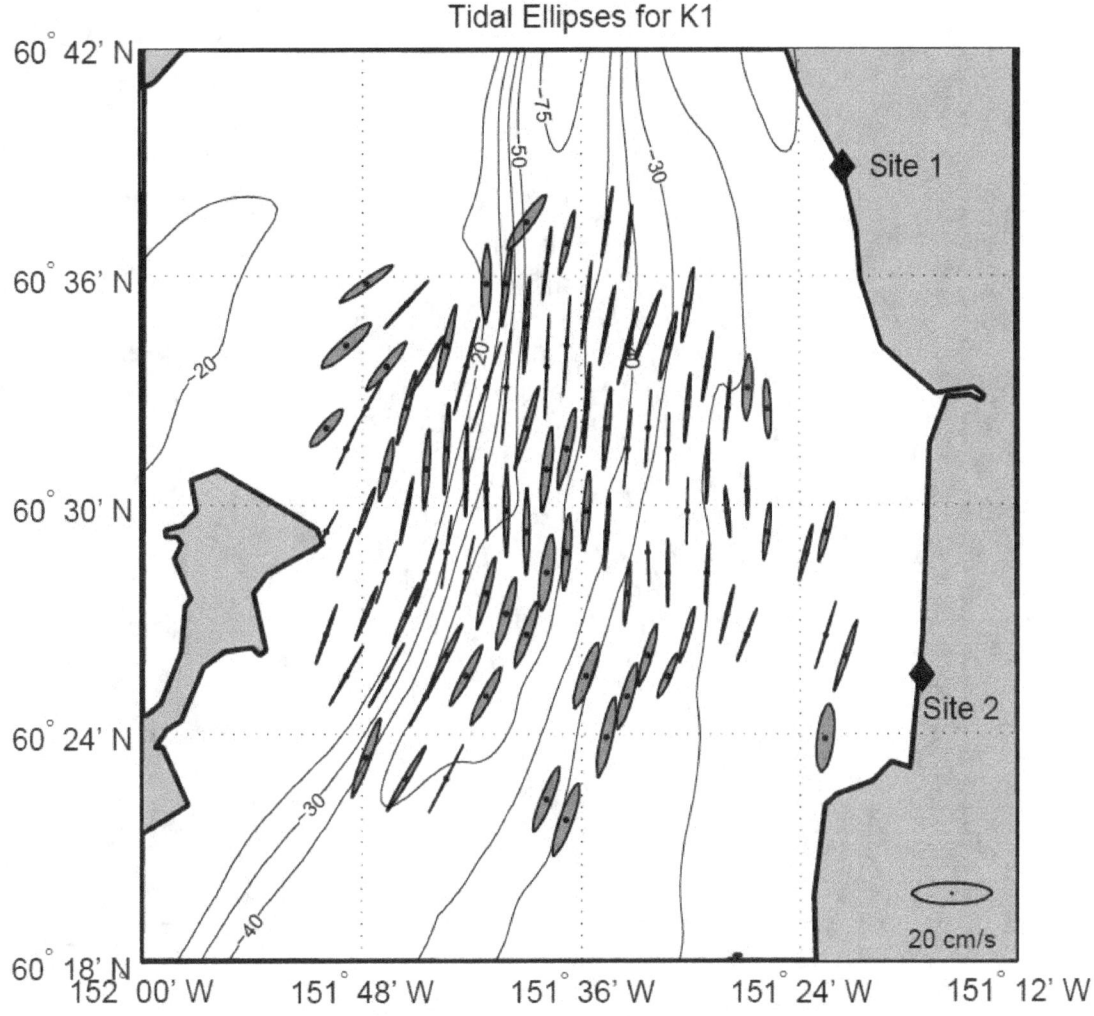

5A

Figures 5: Tidal ellipses for a) K1, b) M2, c) N2 and d) S2 tidal constituents over the whole period. Every fifth grid point is plotted. Bathymetry (m) is indicated by the contour lines.

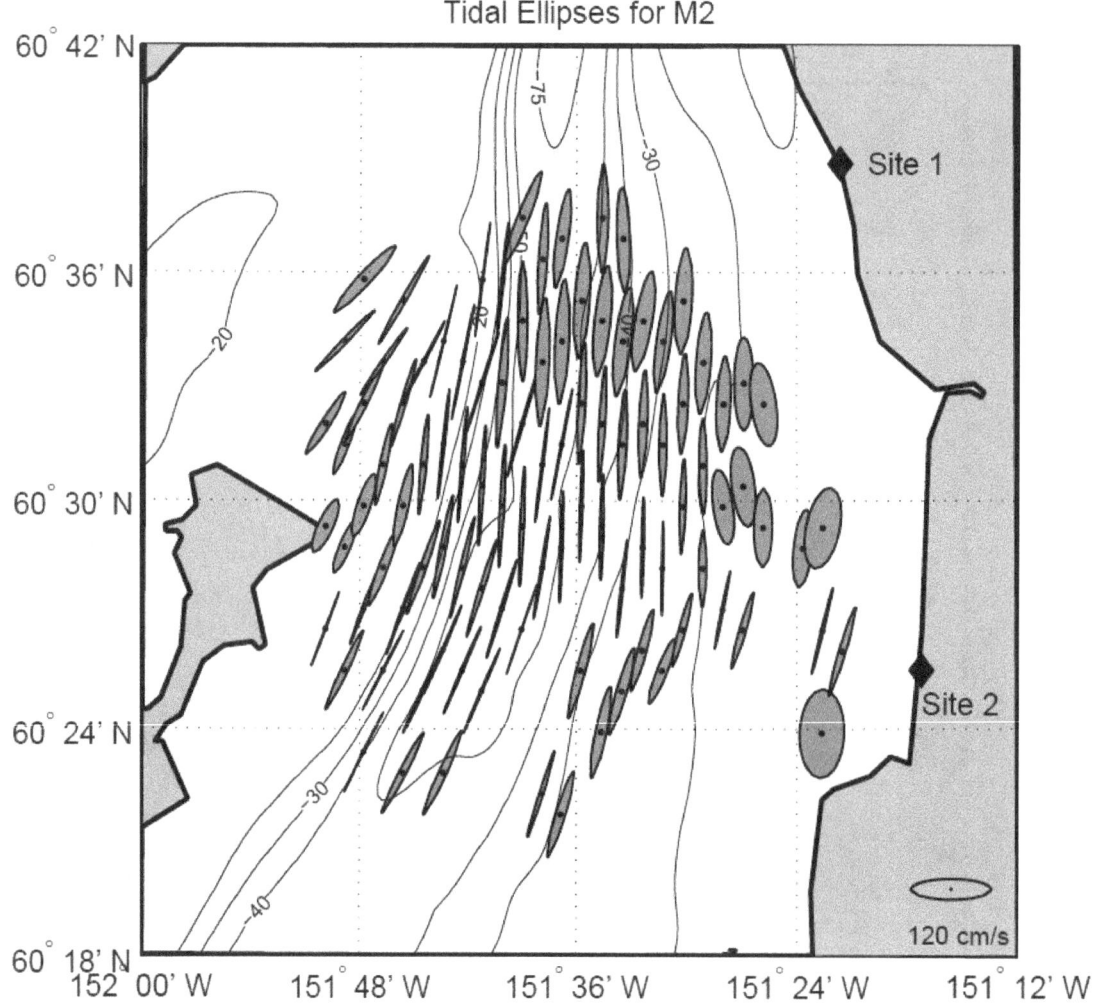

Tidal Ellipses for M2

5B

14

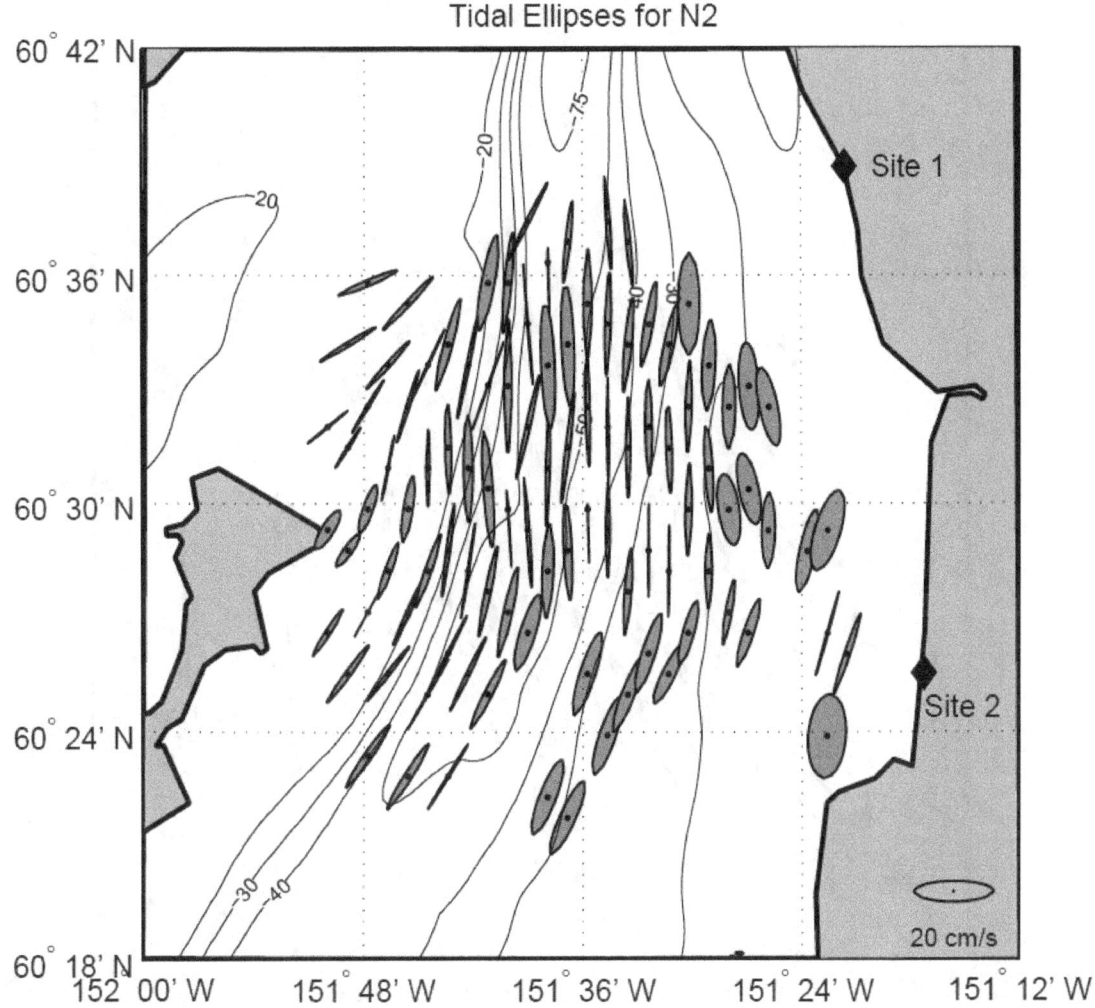

Tidal Ellipses for N2

5C

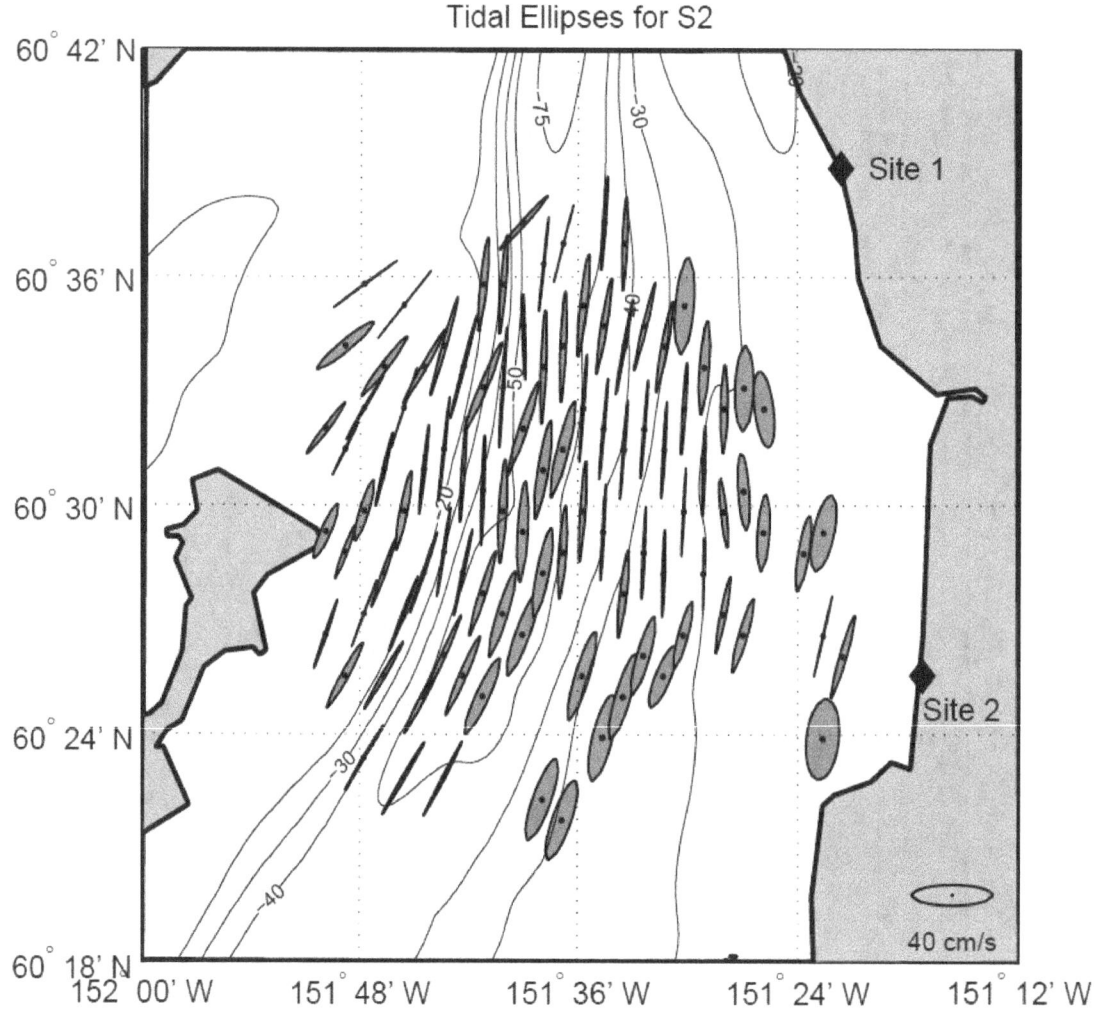

Tidal Ellipses for S2

5D

16

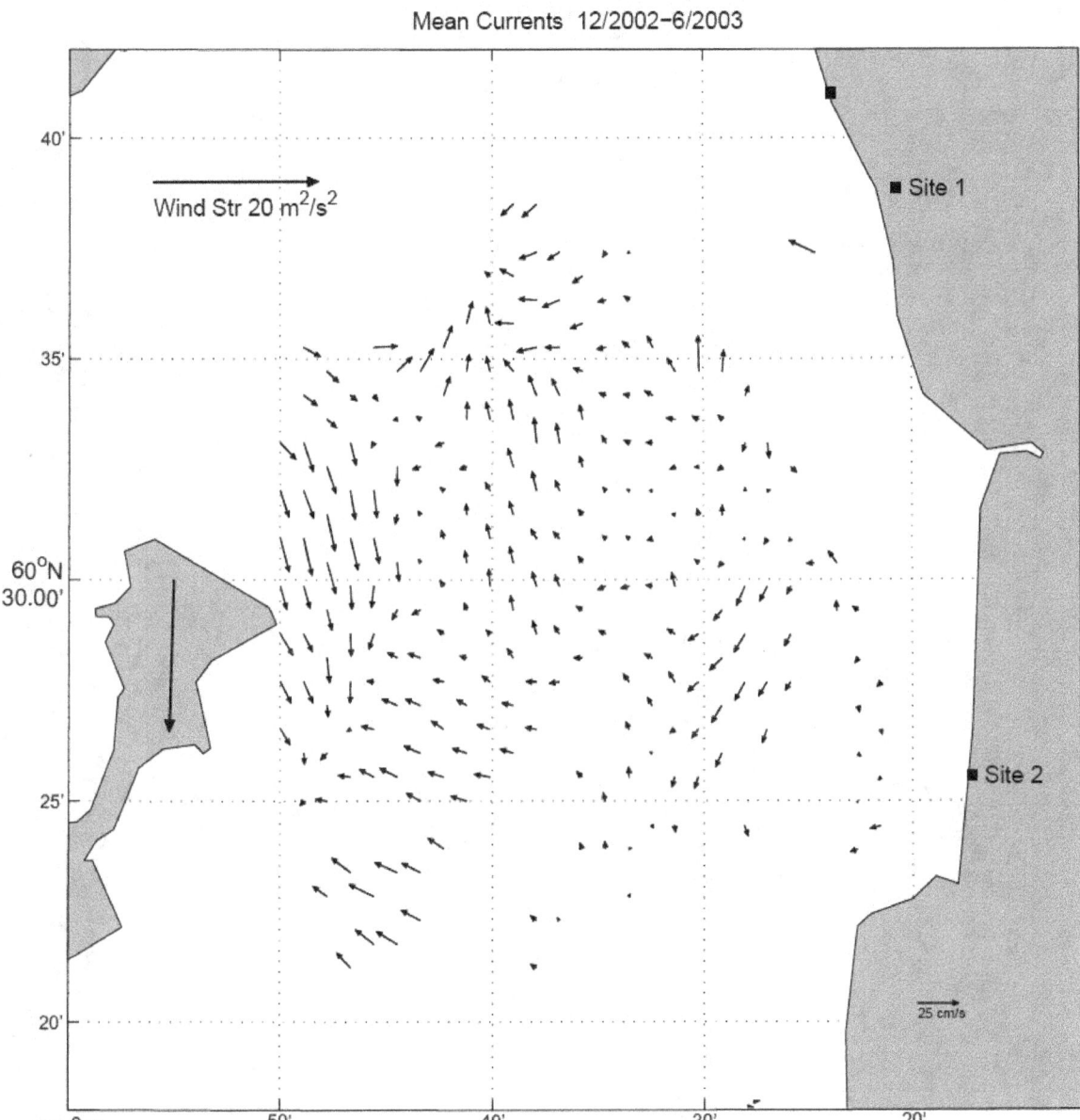

6A

Figures 6: Mean currents for a) the whole period, b) March and c) May. The surface current velocity scale is given in the lower right corner. The arrow on Kalgin Island gives the pseudo wind stress (magnitude = wind velocity squared, direction = wind direction). The scale for the wind stress magnitude is given in the upper left.

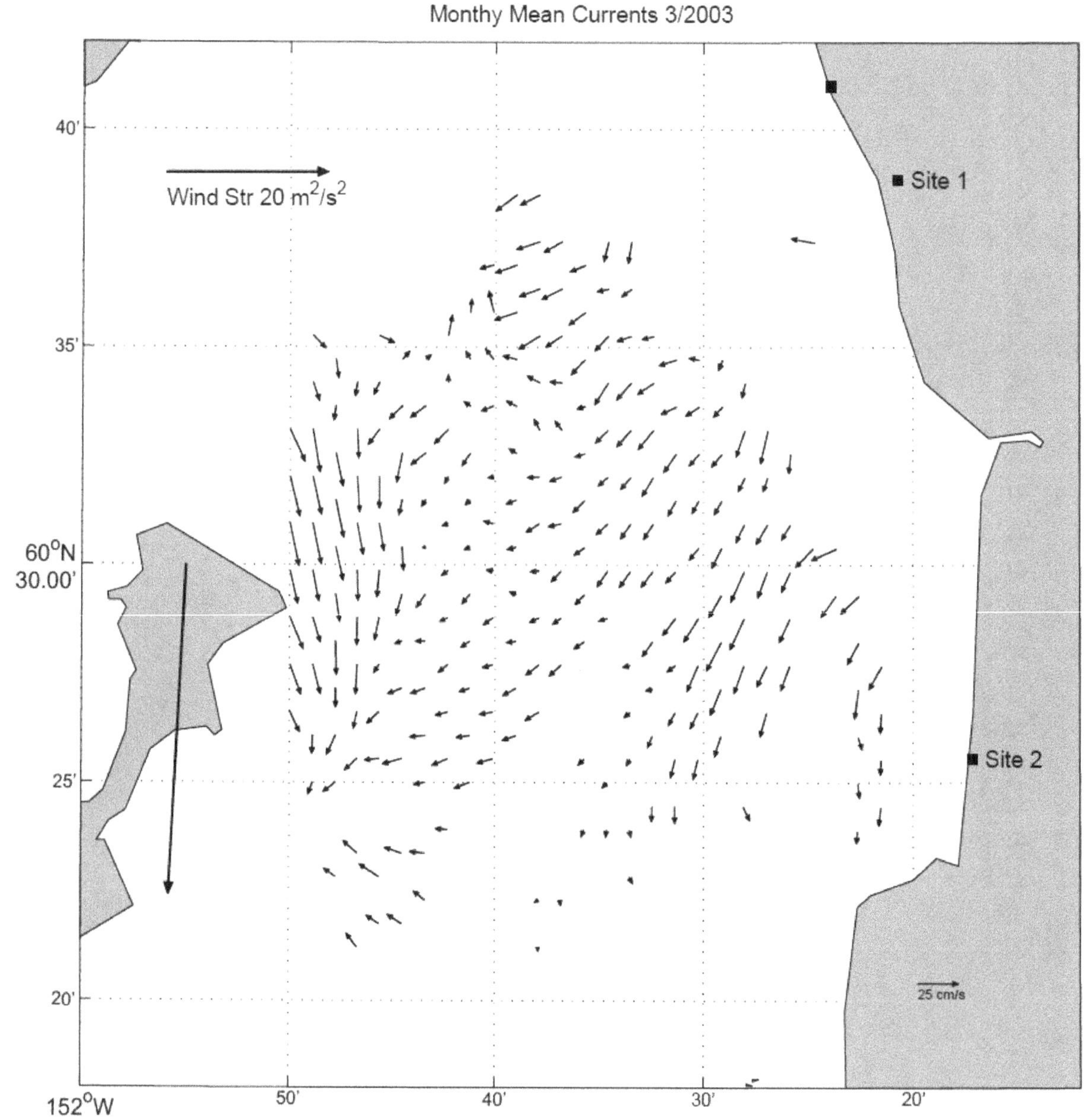
Monthy Mean Currents 3/2003
Wind Str 20 m²/s²
Site 1
Site 2
25 cm/s
40'
35'
60°N
30.00'
25'
20'
152°W
50'
40'
30'
20'

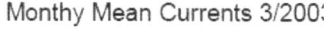

6B

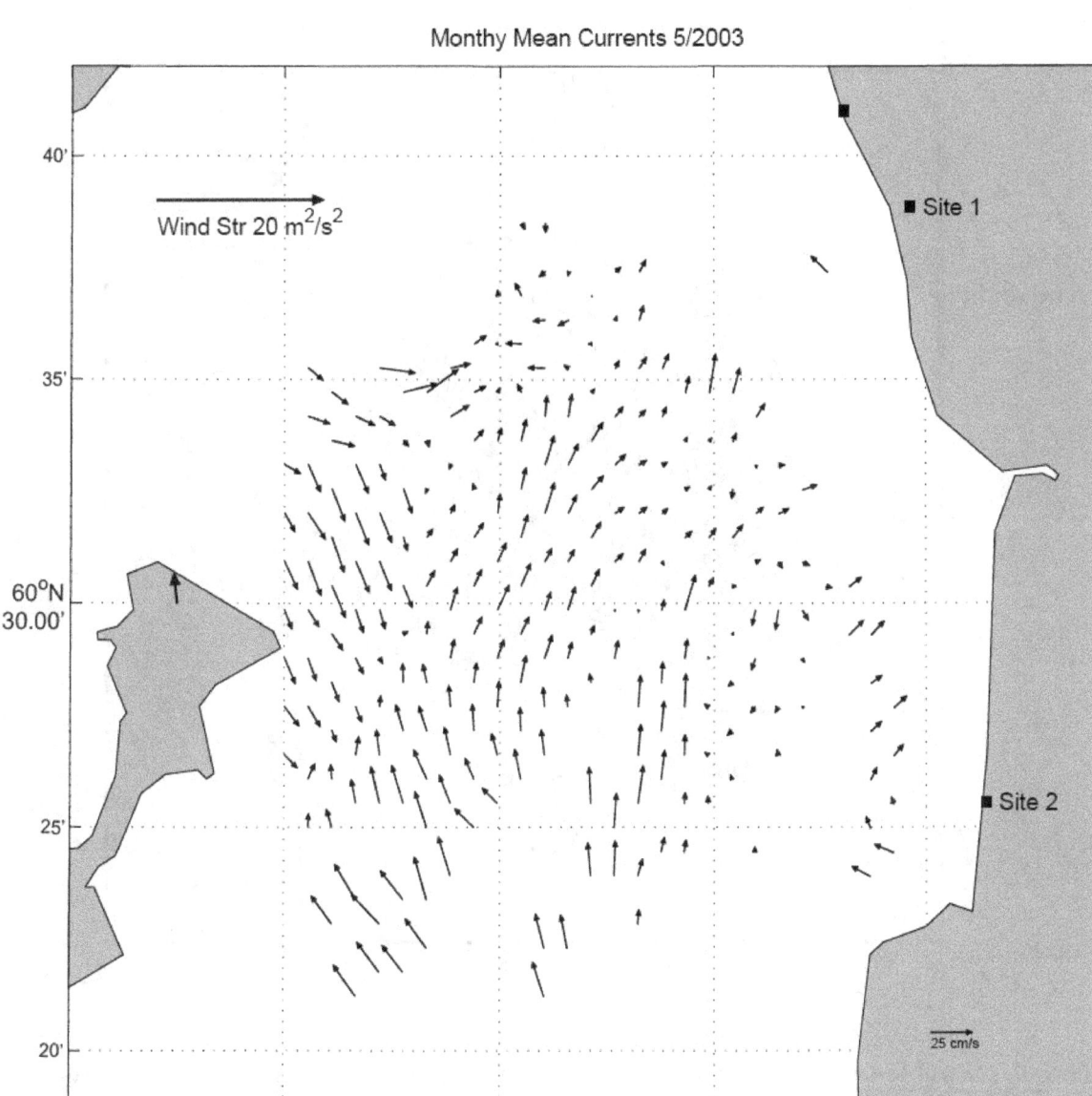

Monthly Mean Currents 5/2003

6C

19

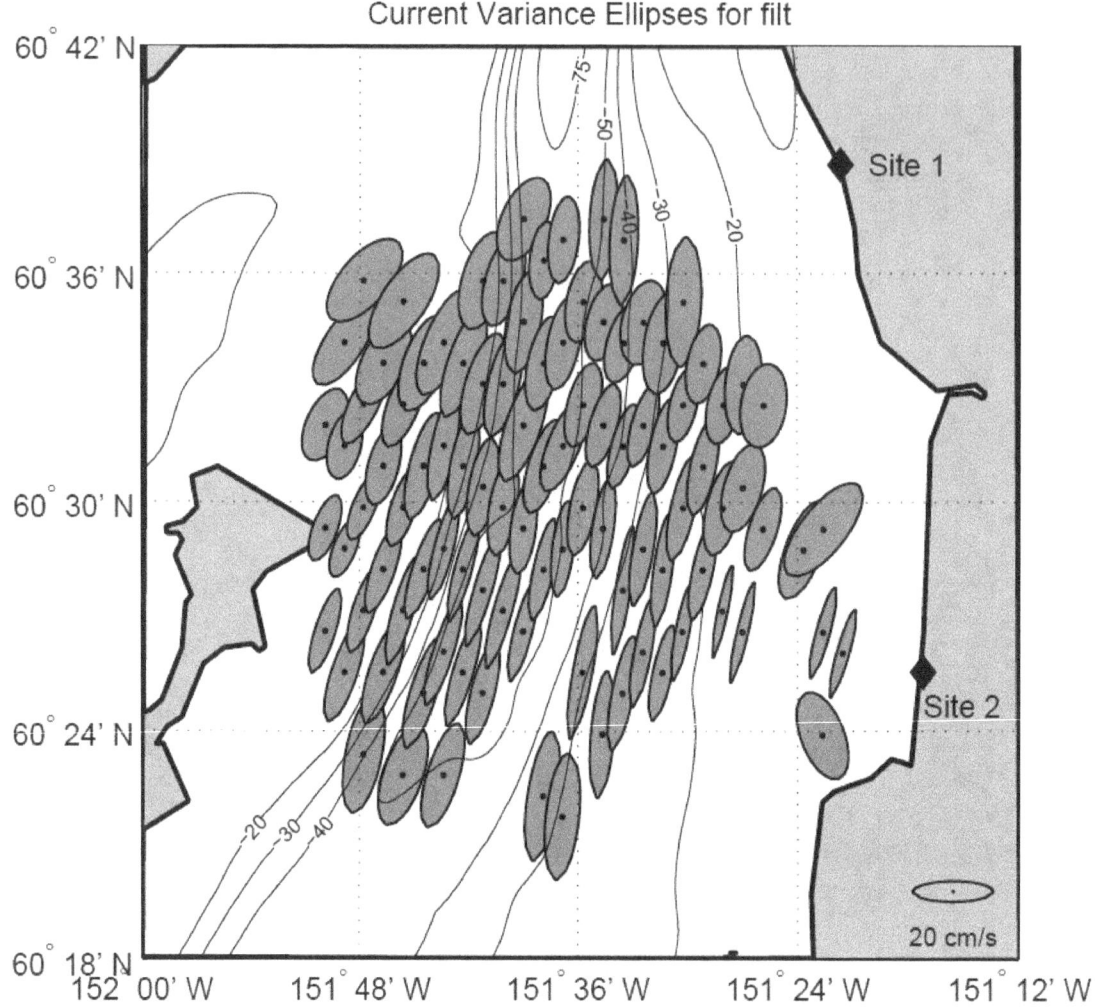

Figure 7: Current variance ellipses plotted over bathymetry contours. The principal axes of the subtidal current variability are polarized along the axis of the inlet with major axis magnitudes ranging between 20 and 40 cm s[-1]. A scale is found in the lower right corner

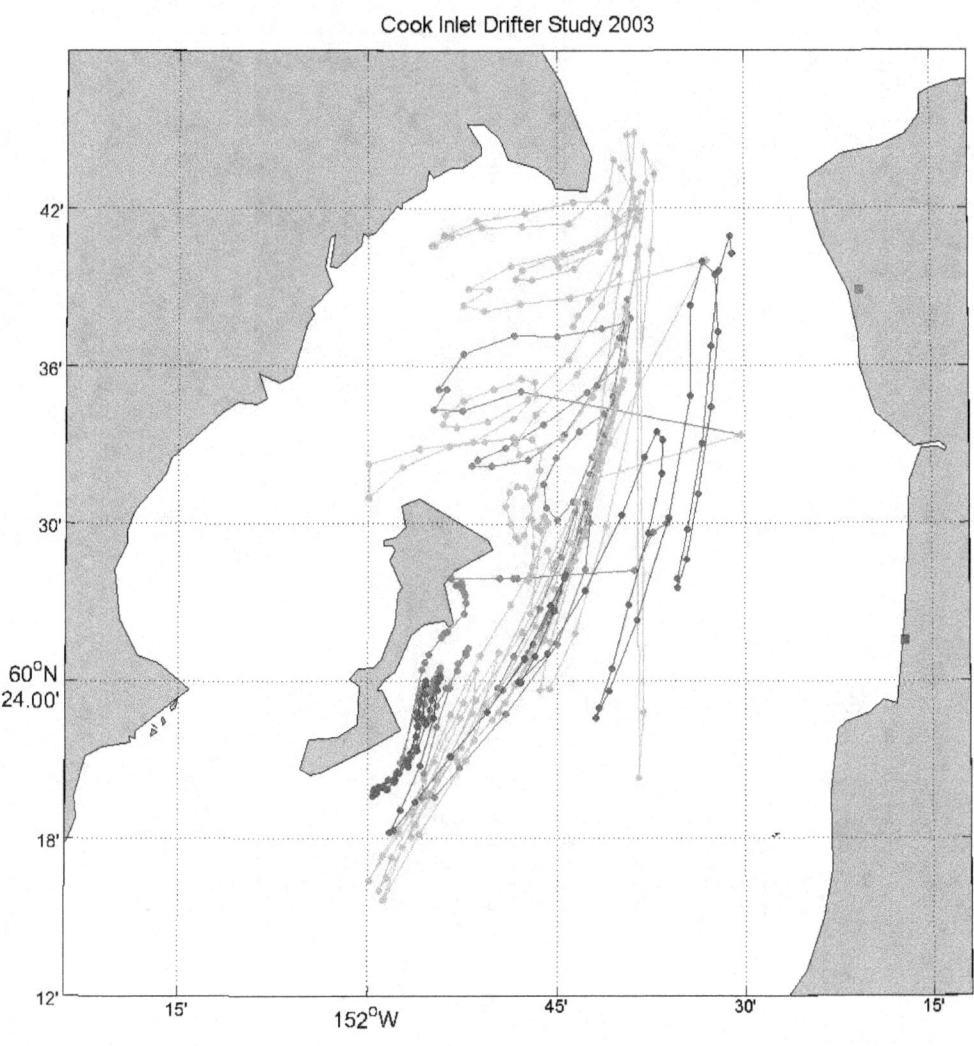

Figure 8: Drifter trajectories for three drifters deployed in Cook Inlet during the HF radar experiment, 2003.

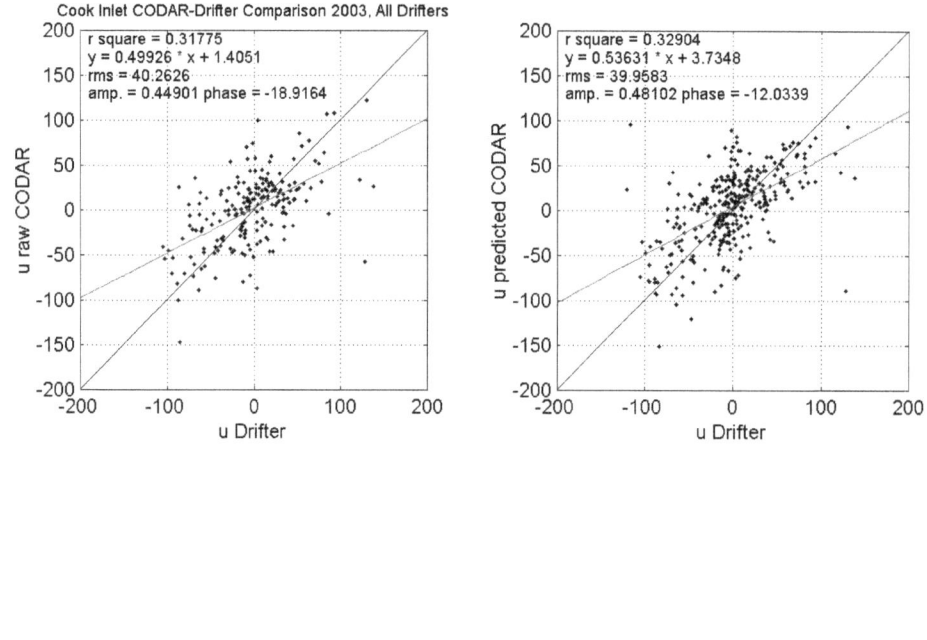

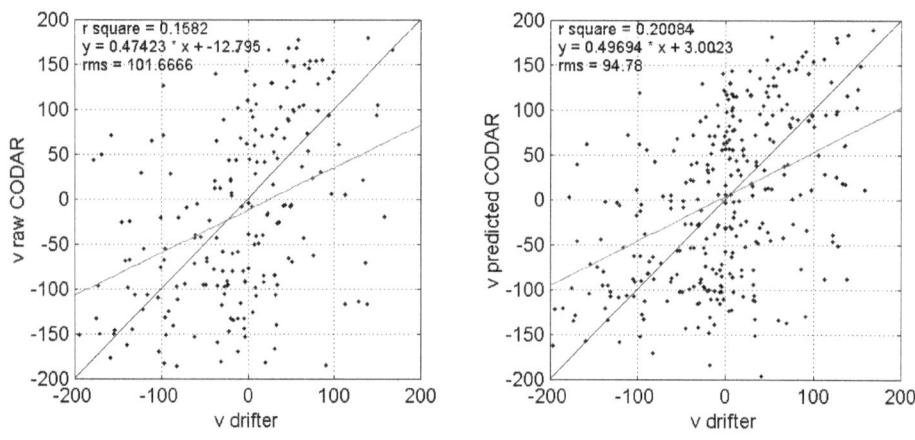

Figure 9: Scatter plot of the drifter-HF radar velocity comparison. The upper (lower) figures give the regression of the HF radar velocities against the drifters for the longitudinal (meridional) velocities. The figures on the left are based on the predicted velocities based on the tidal predictions from the tidal analysis, and the figures on the right are for the actual HF radar data.

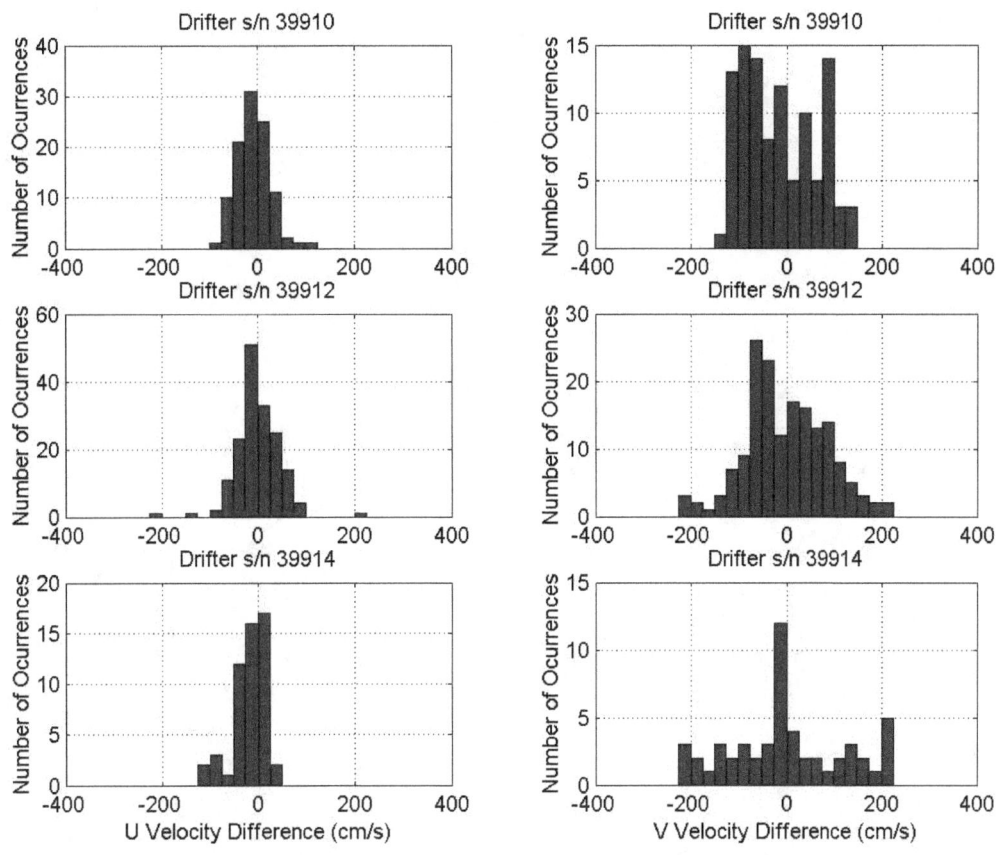

Figure 10: Histograms of velocity component differences between HF radar and six drifter-derived currents in Cook Inlet study.